TELESCOPES FOR KIDS

TELESCOPES FOR KIDS

A JUNIOR SCIENTIST'S GUIDE
to Stargazing, Constellations, and Discovering Far-Off Galaxies

VANESSA THOMAS

ROCKRIDGE PRESS

To my parents and sisters, who support me whenever I reach for a new star. To my niece and nephew, who inspired me to write this book.

Copyright © 2021 by Rockridge Press, Emeryville, California

No part of this publication may be reproduced, stored in a retrieval system, or transmitted in any form or by any means, electronic, mechanical, photocopying, recording, scanning, or otherwise, except as permitted under Sections 107 or 108 of the 1976 United States Copyright Act, without the prior written permission of the Publisher. Requests to the Publisher for permission should be addressed to the Permissions Department, Rockridge Press, 6005 Shellmound Street, Suite 175, Emeryville, CA 94608.

Limit of Liability/Disclaimer of Warranty: The Publisher and the author make no representations or warranties with respect to the accuracy or completeness of the contents of this work and specifically disclaim all warranties, including without limitation warranties of fitness for a particular purpose. No warranty may be created or extended by sales or promotional materials. The advice and strategies contained herein may not be suitable for every situation. This work is sold with the understanding that the Publisher is not engaged in rendering medical, legal, or other professional advice or services. If professional assistance is required, the services of a competent professional person should be sought. Neither the Publisher nor the author shall be liable for damages arising herefrom. The fact that an individual, organization, or website is referred to in this work as a citation and/or potential source of further information does not mean that the author or the Publisher endorses the information the individual, organization, or website may provide or recommendations they/it may make. Further, readers should be aware that websites listed in this work may have changed or disappeared between when this work was written and when it is read.

For general information on our other products and services or to obtain technical support, please contact our Customer Care Department within the United States at (866) 744-2665, or outside the United States at (510) 253-0500.

Rockridge Press publishes its books in a variety of electronic and print formats. Some content that appears in print may not be available in electronic books, and vice versa.

TRADEMARKS: Rockridge Press and the Rockridge Press logo are trademarks or registered trademarks of Callisto Media Inc. and/or its affiliates, in the United States and other countries, and may not be used without written permission. All other trademarks are the property of their respective owners. Rockridge Press is not associated with any product or vendor mentioned in this book.

Series Designer: Junior Scientist Design Team
Interior and Cover Designer: Mando Daniel
Art Producer: Tom Hood
Editor: Erum Khan
Production Editor: Andrew Yackira

Illustrations © Conor Buckley, 2020. Photographs © iStock, cover; Ridofranz/iStock, pp viii, 1; NASA/Science Source, p. 2; Shutterstock, pp 3, 12, 13, 50, 53; peepo/iStock, p. 18; Alan Dyer/VWPics/Alamy p. 35; Cristian Cestaro/Alamy, p. 40; Nikita Roytman/Alamy p. 42; AarStudio/iStock, p. 47; NASA, p. 49; John Chumack/Science Source, pp 51, 55, 56, 57; John Sanford/Science Source, p. 52; Babak Tafreshi/ Science Source, p. 54; Photo illustration courtesy Laura Skinner, cover.

Author Photo courtesy of Teresa Thomas.

ISBN: Print 978-1-64739-824-8 | eBook 978-1-64739-999-3
R1
Printed in China

CONTENTS

WELCOME, JUNIOR SCIENTIST!

I was a kid like you when I fell in love with the **stars**.

My family went camping a lot, and at night, we would sit around the campfire and look up. We pointed out **satellites**, which looked like stars that slowly moved across the sky, and we counted **meteors** to find out who could see the most. When I was 10, I saw my very first **comet**! After my uncle gave me a book about **constellations**, I started trying to match the star patterns in my book to the real ones up above.

One time when we were camping, I remember seeing a green glow in the sky. It was the **northern lights**! They were beautiful and fascinating. I became very curious. I wanted to know what the lights were and what made them shine.

When I started reading and learning more, I found out that there are people called astronomers who study the stars, comets, and even the northern lights to find out what they are and how they formed. Astronomers often observe things that are very far away, but what they learn teaches us more about ourselves, our **planet**, and our place in the big **universe** that we're all a part of. I decided I wanted to study astronomy myself.

Are you curious about the stars, constellations, planets, comets, and other things in space? Well, you can become an astronomer, too! This book will get you started. We'll talk about different types of things you can see in the night sky and how to find them. Are you ready, budding astronomer? Let's start exploring!

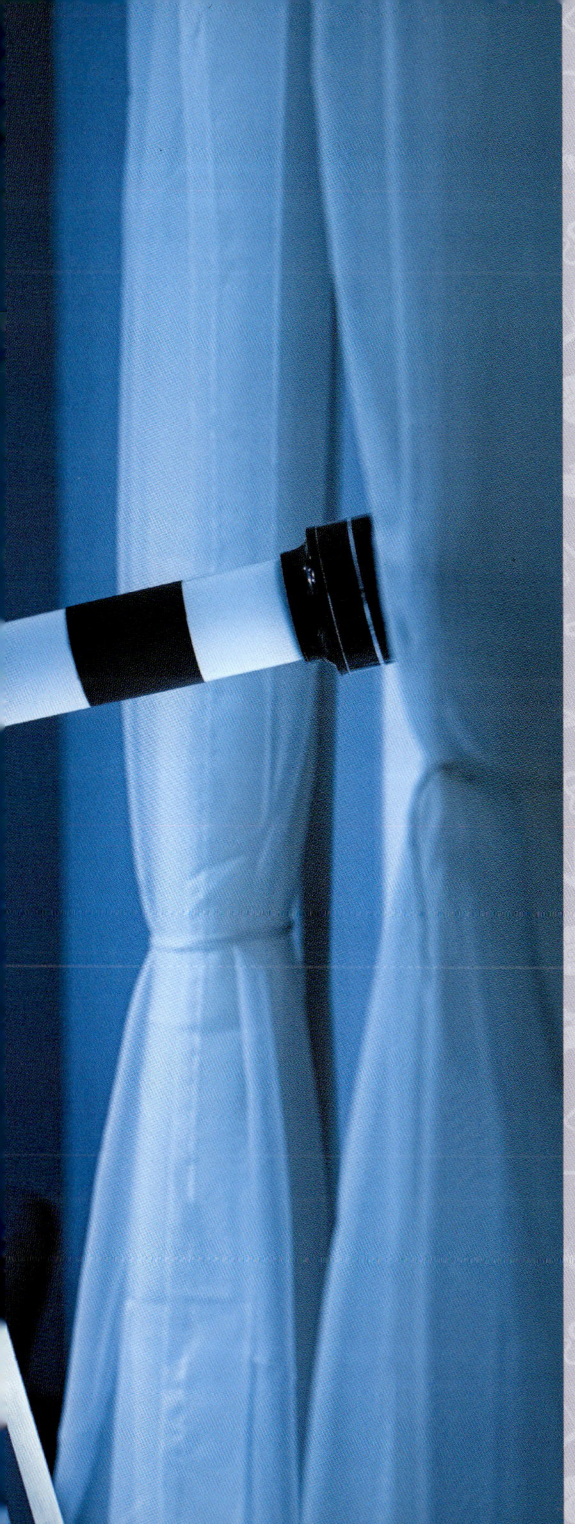

PART ONE

WHAT IS ASTRONOMY?

Astronomy is the study of objects in the sky—everything beyond Earth's **atmosphere**. That includes the **Sun** and **Moon** as well as stars, other planets, **asteroids**, comets, **galaxies**, and more. You can do astronomy with just your eyes, by watching and learning how things look or move in the sky. But to discover more, you can use tools like binoculars or telescopes.

When you look at stars or other things in the sky just for fun, whether or not you learn something new, that's called stargazing.

The Night Sky

The universe is bigger than you can probably imagine! It is filled with stars, planets, galaxies, and more waiting for you to explore.

GALAXIES, NEAR AND FAR

A galaxy is a huge collection of stars, **gas**, and dust. We live in a galaxy called the Milky Way. Our Sun is one of billions of stars in the Milky Way. The universe is home to billions of galaxies.

There are different kinds of galaxies with their own shapes and sizes. The Milky Way is a spiral galaxy. It has a pinwheel structure, with "arms" full of stars that curl around the galaxy's center.

Other galaxies have no spiral arms. Elliptical galaxies are round or egg shaped. Irregular galaxies look messy, with no real shape at all.

THE LIFE OF A STAR

Stars are large, glowing balls of gas held together by **gravity**. Even though they're not alive, stars are like living things because they are born, they live for a while, and then they die. Stars form when gravity pulls a lot of gas together really tightly, causing the gas to create light and heat. Stars shine for millions or even billions of years. But when the gas runs out, a star dies. Smaller stars fade away gently, but big stars explode and create **supernovae**!

TIME IN SPACE

When you look at the night sky, you're looking back in time! The universe is so big, it takes time for light from planets, stars, and galaxies to get to us. The starlight we see tonight actually left the stars many years ago. We see the stars as they appeared back then. The farther away something is, the longer it takes its light to reach us (and the farther back in time we see).

In space, we measure big distances in **light-years**. Light from a star that is 100 light-years away took 100 years to reach us. We see how it looked 100 years ago.

Stories in the Stars

Long ago, people looked up at the stars and saw patterns. They gave the stars and star patterns names based on people, tools, animals, gods, and monsters from stories in their culture. Sometimes they made up new stories about the stars and the patterns they formed.

People from different cultures have their own stories, including the Greeks, Romans, Chinese, Egyptians, Aboriginal Australians, and Native Americans. So the same stars and star patterns often have unique names in different parts of the world.

Today, large patterns of stars are known as constellations. Modern-day astronomers divided the sky into 88 official constellations and decided which names to use.

Some groups of stars form shapes but are not official constellations. They are called **asterisms**. You might have heard of one: the Big Dipper. It is part of the constellation Ursa Major, the Great Bear.

Astronomy Basics

Here are some tips to help you become more familiar with the sky and figure out what you can observe.

SEARCHING BY SEASON

You've probably noticed that when the seasons change, many things outside change. Well, the same is true for the night sky! Different stars and constellations appear at different times of the year.

In this book, here's how we define each season in the Northern Hemisphere (north of Earth's equator).

Spring – March, April, May

Summer – June, July, August

Fall – September, October, November

Winter – December, January, February

In the Southern Hemisphere (south of the equator), the seasons are the opposite of the Northern Hemisphere. When it's winter in the Northern Hemisphere, it's summer in the Southern Hemisphere. A stargazer in the Southern Hemisphere can also see some different stars and constellations than someone in the Northern Hemisphere can. This book explains how to find things in the Northern skies, but check out page 37 for a sneak peek at some Southern views!

FINDING YOUR WAY AROUND

The Sun, Moon, and stars rise in the east and set in the west. To find those points, face the direction where the Sun's glow is just after sunset. That's west. Lift your arms so your body makes a *T* shape. Your right hand points north. Your left hand points south. East is behind you. You are a human compass!

If it is already dark outside, you can use the North Star, Polaris (page 16). The North Star is always in the north. When you face it, west is on your left, east is on your right, and south is behind you.

Distance across the sky is measured in **degrees**. There are 360 degrees in a circle. If you hold your arm out and make a fist, your fist is about 10 degrees wide.

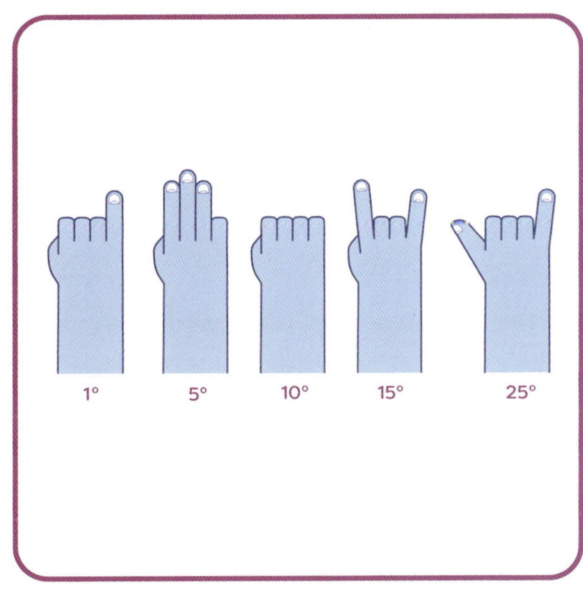

TALK LIKE AN ASTRONOMER

Astronomers use a number called **magnitude** to describe the brightness of a star (or of other objects in the sky). It might seem backward, but bright objects have low numbers and dim ones have high numbers. So a star with a magnitude of 1 is brighter than a star with a magnitude of 6. Really bright objects have negative numbers. Sirius, the brightest star in our night sky, has a magnitude of −1.5!

Many fuzzy-looking objects in the sky, such as galaxies, **nebulae**, and **star clusters**, also have names that use the letter *M* and a number. (For example, the Orion Nebula is M42.) The *M* stands for Messier ("MEZ-ee-ay"), after French comet hunter Charles Messier. He recorded over 100 fuzzy objects that looked like comets but weren't. These are the Messier objects.

What You Need to Start Stargazing

There are many ways to enjoy the night sky, and different tools to explore it.

JUST YOUR EYES

You can observe plenty of objects in the night sky with just your eyes. For example, the Moon, Venus, Jupiter, Mars, Saturn, and Mercury are easy to spot. With a dark sky, you can even view the Milky Way, nearby galaxies, and bright nebulae without equipment.

Some things are best seen with nothing but your eyes. For example, meteors (also called "shooting stars") and **meteor showers** are enjoyed most when you just look up.

COMPASS

A compass is a tool that helps you find directions. You can use a real compass with a needle that points to the direction you're facing, or you can use an app on a smartphone or tablet.

Either way, hold the compass flat in front of you. Turn slowly until the direction you want is at the top, farthest away from you.

RED FLASHLIGHT

"Night vision" helps you see faint objects in the sky. Bright lights, especially white ones, ruin that. To get night vision, visit a dark place without bright lights and let your eyes adjust. The longer you wait, the more (and fainter) objects you can see. It takes about 20 minutes for your eyes to adjust, so be patient.

If you need light while stargazing, use a red flashlight. Red light does not affect your night vision as much. You can buy red flashlights from stores that sell astronomy equipment and in some camping stores. Or just make your own! (See page 9.)

BINOCULARS

Binoculars are a great exploration tool, especially for new astronomers. You'd be amazed by what binoculars can reveal! Many bright star clusters, for example, look incredible through binoculars. So does the Moon. (Seriously, get ready to gasp!)

Binoculars are easy to use. No setup required! Just point them at whatever you want a closer look at. It's also fun to scan the sky with binoculars and discover interesting things!

TELESCOPE

The best telescope for you depends on your needs. Some telescopes, called reflectors, use mirrors to collect and **focus** light. Others, called refractors, use lenses (curved pieces of glass) to focus light. Refractors tend to be long and skinny, while reflectors are shorter and wider.

Some telescopes must be moved by hand to point at targets in the sky. Others use computers to automatically find an object you tell them to focus on. Telescopes that you move by hand are often easier to set up and are great if you know how to locate your target. But you have to keep moving the telescope to follow an object as it travels across the sky. Computerized telescopes track an object once you've found it, but they require power and can take longer to set up.

Telescopes come in all sizes. Those with bigger mirrors or lenses collect more light, making it easier to see faint things in the sky. Big telescopes might show you more objects in better detail, but they are usually heavier and harder to move or set up.

For junior astronomers, I suggest starting small. Small telescopes can show you everything in this book. After you've become an expert telescope user and want to see even more, perhaps then you can upgrade to a bigger telescope.

Many astronomy clubs and observatories let people come look through their big telescopes for free. Search online to find an observatory or astronomy club in your area and see if they hold open houses.

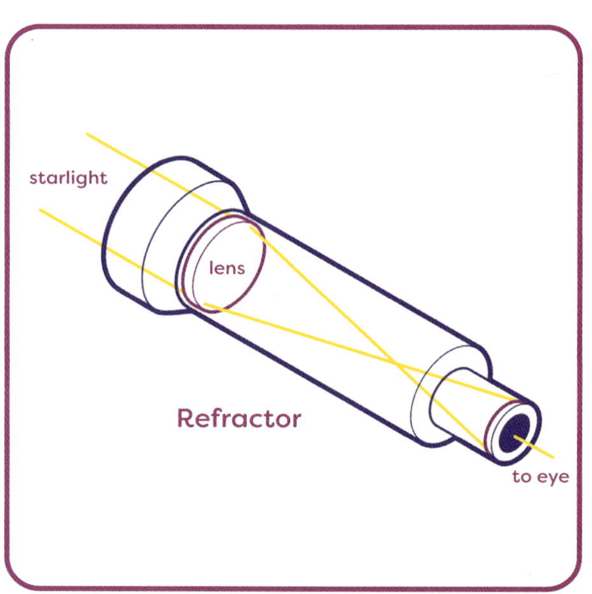

Setting Up Your Telescope

Ready to start using your telescope? Let's go over a telescope's parts and what they do.

The main part of a telescope is the tube that holds the mirrors or lenses, which gather and focus light from the universe. The tube holds these mirrors or lenses in place and helps protect them.

A mount holds the telescope tube and keeps it steady. It can be a big, boxy base. Or it can be a *U*-shaped "fork" or smaller piece that sits on a tripod or a column called a pier.

When setting up your telescope, you might need to put the tube on the mount. For some telescopes, the tube always stays on the mount. If that's true for yours, you can skip this step.

On the outside of the tube is a finder scope. It might look like a smaller

MAKE YOUR OWN RED FLASHLIGHT

Here are two ways to turn a regular flashlight into a red flashlight with the help of an adult: (1) Find a piece of red cellophane or cloth, put it over the front of the flashlight, and attach it with a rubber band. (2) Use red nail polish to paint the front of your flashlight red. You may need multiple layers to get it red enough. It should look like a car's brake light.

telescope. That's exactly what it is! The finder scope gives you a slightly bigger view of the sky than your telescope does. It helps you find things in the sky and aim your telescope at what you want to observe.

Some finder scopes come off when you store your telescope. So you might need to attach and align it when you set up your telescope.

Another important part of your telescope is the eyepiece. This is what you look through. It focuses light into your eye. You can remove eyepieces and change them. Eyepieces have different sizes that give different **magnifications**. In fact, it's the eyepiece that magnifies, not the telescope! Eyepieces with low numbers, such as 10 mm, show a smaller part of the sky but magnify more. Eyepieces with larger numbers, such as 40 mm, show a bigger part of the sky but magnify less.

Near the eyepiece is the focuser. It's a knob you turn to focus your view when looking through the eyepiece. If you wear glasses, you can take them off and use this knob to get the focus just right.

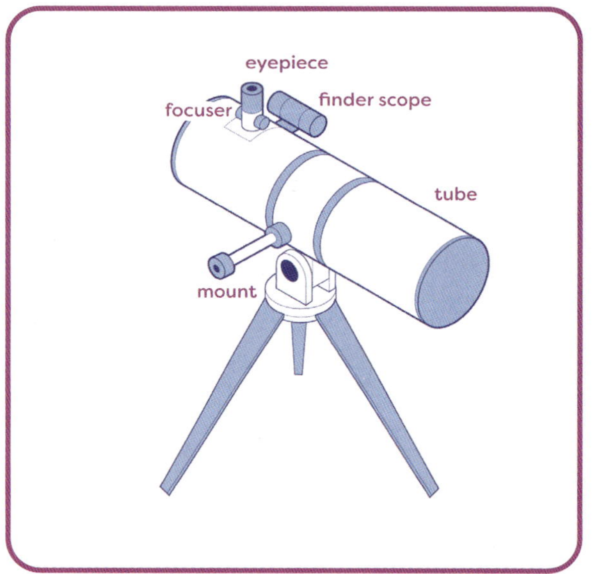

Tips and Tricks to Get Started

Before you start stargazing, there are some key things you'll want to plan for. Ask a parent or another adult for help.

Look for clear skies. Clouds can block your view. If there are only a few clouds in the sky, you can view objects peeking out from between them. (But clouds might move in front of something as you're observing it!)

Pick a good spot. The best place is a safe, dark, open space. Set up as far as you can from any lights and away from buildings or trees that will block your view of the sky. Large backyards, parks, sports fields, or open spaces in the country are great. (Just make sure you have permission to be there at night!) Also, try to set up away from roads so car headlights don't shine in your eyes.

Find flat ground. When you are using a telescope, you'll want to make sure it doesn't tip over! If possible, set it up before it gets dark. It's easier to see what you're doing if there's still some daylight. Remember not to point your telescope at the Sun, though, unless you have a solar filter.

Dress for the weather. Bring more warm clothing than you think you'll need. It can get cold when you're outside for a long time!

Plan ahead. What's visible in the sky depends on what time it is. Use star maps, a **planisphere**, sky program, or app to see what you can observe before you go outside. (See page 58 for examples.) Bring a small table to put your maps or planisphere on, and use your red flashlight to read them.

Don't give up. Finding faint objects in the sky can be hard, even for adults with lots of experience. It takes skill and practice. Keep trying!

PART TWO

EXPLORE THE NIGHT SKY

Here are 40 great objects to begin exploring in the Northern Hemisphere. Many can also be seen from the Southern Hemisphere.

We'll start with objects you can view year-round (from the Northern Hemisphere). Then, we switch from stars, constellations, and galaxies to planets and moons. Did you know that *planet* means "wanderer" in Greek? That's because planets move relative to the stars. Where they appear changes depending on when you look. To find out when you can see them, check astronomy magazines, websites, apps, or sky-mapping programs. (See More to Discover, page 58.)

Big Dipper

The Big Dipper might be the most famous asterism in the sky. Its stars are bright, and they form a large bowl and handle that are easy to find on clear nights throughout the year.

1. Face north.
2. Look for seven bright stars together. Three stars form a short, bent line next to four stars that form a rectangle shape.
3. The bent part is the handle, and the rectangular part is the bowl. You've found the Big Dipper!

STAR STATS

LOCATION: Ursa Major (ER-sah MAY-jer), the Great Bear

SEASON: Visible all year, but highest in the spring

DIFFICULTY: 1 (Easy)

SPACE FACT: When the Big Dipper is high in the sky, the "open" part of the bowl faces down toward the ground. When it's low (close to the ground), the bowl's opening faces upward.

Mizar and Alcor

SAY IT! *MY-zahr and AL-core*

Look closely at the middle star in the Big Dipper's handle, and you'll see that there are actually two stars there. One is called Mizar and the other is Alcor.

1. Face north and look for the Big Dipper.
2. Find the middle star in the Big Dipper's handle.
3. Look for a dimmer star next to the bright one. That's Alcor. The brighter star is Mizar.

STAR STATS

LOCATION: Ursa Major (ER-sah MAY-jer), the Great Bear

SEASON: Visible all year, but highest in the spring

DIFFICULTY: 1 (Easy)

SPACE FACT: Sometimes a star is actually made up of two or more stars that are too close together to tell apart with just your eyes. If you aim a telescope at Mizar, you'll actually see *two* stars there, in addition to Alcor. Mizar is really made up of four stars in all!

Polaris (the North Star)

SAY IT! *poh-LAIR-iss*

Polaris is also known as the North Star. It's called that because it is located almost exactly at the sky's north pole. It is not the brightest star, but it is easy to find.

1. Face north and look for the Big Dipper.
2. Find the two stars on the outer edge of the Big Dipper's bowl (farthest from the handle).
3. Draw an imaginary line from the star at the bottom of the bowl to the star at the top of the bowl.
4. Keep drawing your straight line away from the Big Dipper's bowl about 25 degrees until you reach another star. That's Polaris!

STAR STATS

LOCATION: Ursa Minor (ER-sah MY-ner), the Little Bear

SEASON: Visible all year

DIFFICULTY: 1 (Easy)

SPACE FACT: If you stood at Earth's North Pole, Polaris would be straight up!

Little Dipper

The Little Dipper is an asterism in the constellation Ursa Minor, the Little Bear. It looks like the Big Dipper, with seven stars forming a handle and bowl, but it is smaller and fainter.

1. Face north and look for Polaris.
2. Polaris is the end of the Little Dipper's handle.
3. Polaris and two other stars form the Little Dipper's curved handle, which leads to four stars forming a rectangle shape, the bowl.

STAR STATS

LOCATION: Ursa Minor (ER-sah MY-ner), the Little Bear

SEASON: Visible all year in the Northern Hemisphere

DIFFICULTY: 2 (Medium)

ORIGIN STORY: The handles of the Big and Little Dippers are the Great and Little Bears' tails. One story says they got stretched out when the Roman god Jupiter threw the bears into the sky by their tails.

THINGS WE CAN'T SEE

Gravity is an invisible force that pulls things together. Earth's gravity holds us to the ground. It's what makes things fall when you let go of them. It's also what keeps the Moon, and satellites we launch into space, in orbit around Earth.

The bigger (or more massive) something is, the more gravity it has. The Sun is much bigger than Earth, so its gravity is stronger. The Sun's gravity holds all of the Solar System's planets in orbit around it. The Moon is smaller than Earth, so if you went there, you would feel less gravity and could jump a lot higher than you can here!

Gravity is what holds together all the stars in the star clusters you see. When you look at a galaxy, know that all the stars in that galaxy are also held together by gravity.

Pinwheel Galaxy (M101)

The Pinwheel Galaxy is a beautiful spiral galaxy that you can find with a small telescope under a dark sky.

1. Look at the two stars at the end of the Big Dipper's handle.
2. Draw an imaginary triangle with three equal sides using the two end stars in the handle and an invisible star between and above them (if you imagine the Big Dipper's bowl opening upward).
3. Aim your telescope where that invisible star would be. When you see a round, fuzzy patch of light, you have found the Pinwheel Galaxy!

STAR STATS

LOCATION: Ursa Major (ER-sah MAY-jer), the Great Bear

SEASON: Visible all year, but highest in the spring

DIFFICULTY: 3 (Hard)

SPACE FACT: The Pinwheel Galaxy is almost twice as big as our Milky Way galaxy. Astronomers think it holds over a trillion stars!

Whirlpool Galaxy (M51)

Stargazers who find the Whirlpool Galaxy with a telescope enjoy stunning views of its spiral arms.

1. Spot the star at the end of the Big Dipper's handle.
2. Imagine the Big Dipper is right-side up (if it isn't already).
3. Look about 10 degrees "below" the star at the end of its handle for another star that's about the same brightness.
4. Point your telescope about one-quarter of the way from the handle star to the other star. The round, fuzzy shape you see is the Whirlpool Galaxy!

STAR STATS

LOCATION: Canes Venatici (KAY-neez veh-NAT-iss-eye), the Hunting Dogs

SEASON: Visible all year, but highest in the spring

DIFFICULTY: 3 (Hard)

SPACE FACT: Look closely and you might see a bright spot at the tip of one of the galaxy's spiral arms. That's actually a smaller galaxy *behind* the Whirlpool!

Arcturus

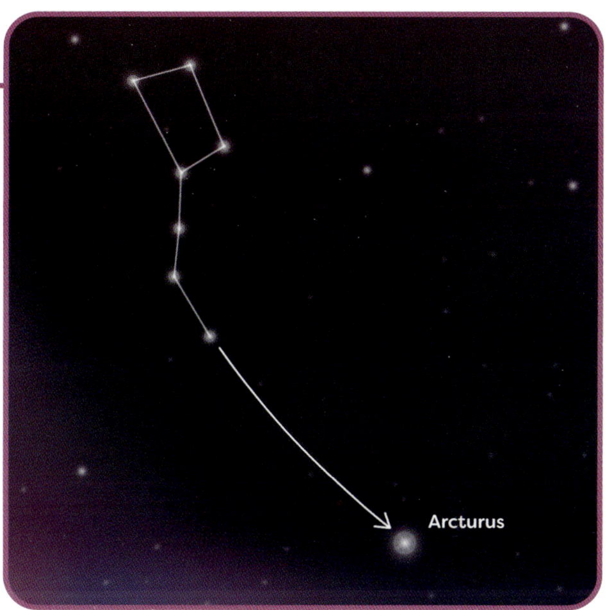

SAY IT! *ark-TOUR-iss*

Arcturus is a large, bright star called a red giant. It is the brightest star in the constellation Boötes, the Herdsman, and the fourth-brightest star in the entire night sky.

1. Face north and look for the Big Dipper.
2. Draw an imaginary curved line through the stars in the handle, from the bowl to the end of the handle.
3. Keep following that curve away from the Big Dipper across the sky until you get to a bright, yellowish star. That's Arcturus!

STAR STATS

LOCATION: Boötes (boh-OH-teez), the Herdsman

SEASON: Spring

DIFFICULTY: 1 (Easy)

SPACE FACT: You can remember how to find Arcturus by remembering the phrase "arc to Arcturus." Just use the Big Dipper's handle to draw an arc to Arcturus.

Spica

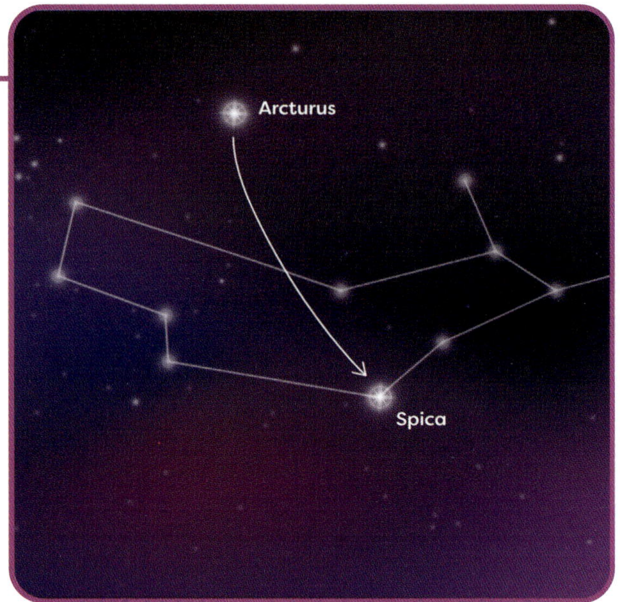

SAY IT! *SPIKE-ah*

Spica is the brightest star in the constellation Virgo, the Maiden. Spica is actually made up of two stars that orbit around each other. But they are so close together, you see them as only one bright star.

1. Face north and look for the Big Dipper.
2. Trace an imaginary curved line through the Big Dipper's handle to Arcturus.
3. Continue tracing that line in the same direction until you get to a bright, blue-colored star. That's Spica!

STAR STATS

LOCATION: Virgo (VUR-go), the Maiden

SEASON: Spring or summer

DIFFICULTY: 1 (Easy)

SPACE FACT: To remember how to find Spica, just remember that first you "arc to Arcturus" and then you "speed on to Spica."

Leo (the Lion)

SAY IT! *LEE-oh*

Leo, the Lion, is a big, bright constellation that, with some imagination, really looks like a lion! Leo's brightest star is Regulus (REH-gyoo-luss), the heart of the Lion. Its second-brightest star is Denebola (deh-NEH-bow-lah), the Lion's tail.

1. Find the Big Dipper.
2. Imagine that the bottom of the Big Dipper's bowl has a hole and is leaking water.
3. Follow the dripping water to a group of bright stars.
4. Look for stars forming the shape of a backward question mark. That's Leo's head and mane. A rectangular group of stars forms the Lion's body. Three bright stars form a triangle, which is Leo's back legs and tail.

STAR STATS

LOCATION: Southern sky

SEASON: Spring

DIFFICULTY: 2 (Medium)

SPACE FACT: Regulus is actually made up of four stars orbiting each other.

The Beehive (Praesepe, M44)

SAY IT! *prih-SEE-pee*

The Beehive star cluster is a large group of over a thousand young stars in our Milky Way galaxy. The group is held together by gravity. You can see the Beehive without any equipment in a clear and very dark sky, but it looks best through binoculars or a small telescope.

1. Face south and look for Leo.
2. Look in the direction that Leo is facing (ahead of, or to the right of, his head), about 15 degrees away from Leo.
3. Search for a faint, cloudy patch of light. That's the Beehive!

STAR STATS

LOCATION: Cancer (CAN-sir), the Crab

SEASON: Spring

DIFFICULTY: 2 (Medium)

SPACE FACT: Astronomers have discovered planets orbiting some of the stars in the Beehive.

Vega

SAY IT! *VAY-gah*

Vega is one of the brightest stars of the summer night sky. It is the brightest star in the constellation Lyra, the Harp.

1. Late in the evening on summer nights, look high in the sky, almost overhead.
2. Look for the brightest star in the area, which might look bluish-white. That's Vega.

STAR STATS

LOCATION: Lyra (LIE-rah), the Harp

SEASON: Summer

DIFFICULTY: 1 (Easy)

SPACE FACT: Because Earth's axis wobbles slowly over thousands of years, Vega was once the North Star! And it will be again thousands of years from now.

ZODIAC CONSTELLATIONS

There are 13 constellations that are known as zodiac constellations. These are constellations that the Sun appears in during the year. The Sun spends about a month in each zodiac constellation as it moves through the sky.

The path that the Sun takes through the sky during the year is called the **ecliptic**. The 13 zodiac constellations all appear along the ecliptic. Fun fact: the Moon and the planets in our Solar System also travel along the ecliptic!

When the Sun is in one of these constellations, you cannot observe that constellation at night (because it sets with the Sun). Some of the zodiac constellations have bright stars and are easy to find, but others are faint and very hard to find.

These are the 13 zodiac constellations:

SAGITTARIUS, THE ARCHER
CAPRICORN, THE GOAT
AQUARIUS, THE WATER BEARER
PISCES, THE FISH
ARIES, THE RAM
TAURUS, THE BULL
GEMINI, THE TWINS
CANCER, THE CRAB
LEO, THE LION
VIRGO, THE MAIDEN
LIBRA, THE SCALES
SCORPIUS, THE SCORPION
OPHIUCHUS, THE SERPENT

Lyra (the Harp)

SAY IT! *LIE-rah*

Lyra, the Harp, is a small constellation, but it's home to one of the brightest stars in our night sky, Vega, as well as the Ring Nebula.

1. Find Vega, high overhead in the late evening.
2. Look for four fainter stars near Vega that seem to form a long, slanted rectangle (or parallelogram). Vega and those stars make up the Harp, or Lyra.

STAR STATS

LOCATION: High overhead

SEASON: Summer

DIFFICULTY: 2 (Medium)

SPACE FACT: The Ring Nebula (M57) lies almost exactly in between the two stars at the bottom of the Harp, farthest away from Vega. Aim your telescope at it and you'll see a tiny, faint, smoky-looking ring.

Summer Triangle

The Summer Triangle is a large, triangle-shaped asterism appearing in the sky all summer long. It is made up of three bright stars in three different constellations. These stars are Vega, Deneb, and Altair.

1. In the evening during the summer, look high in the sky to find Vega.
2. Look for another bright star about 20 degrees away from Vega, toward the northeastern **horizon**. That's Deneb.
3. Look for a third bright star about 25 degrees away from Vega, toward the southeastern horizon. That's Altair.
4. Draw an imaginary triangle between the three bright stars. That's the Summer Triangle.

STAR STATS

LOCATION: High in the eastern sky

SEASON: Summer

DIFFICULTY: 1 (Easy)

SPACE FACT: While the Summer Triangle is easiest to find throughout the summer, you can spot it in the spring and fall, too.

Northern Cross

The Northern Cross is another large, easy-to-find asterism in the summer sky. It is part of the constellation Cygnus, the Swan. The cross traces the bird's body and outstretched wings.

1. Look for the Summer Triangle.
2. Find Deneb, the bright star of the triangle to the left of Vega.
3. Deneb is the top of the Northern Cross. Three other stars form a line with Deneb. That's the long part of the cross, the Swan's body.
4. Another line of bright stars cuts across the Swan's body, forming the other part of the cross—the Swan's wings.

STAR STATS

LOCATION: Cygnus (SIG-nuss), the Swan

SEASON: Summer

DIFFICULTY: 1 (Easy)

SPACE FACT: *Deneb* means "tail" in Arabic. That star is the Swan's tail. The bottom part of the cross is the Swan's neck and head.

Albireo

SAY IT! *AL-BEER-ee-oh*

Albireo is the head of Cygnus, the Swan. It appears to be one star when you look at it with just your eyes. But aim a telescope at it, and you'll see that it's actually two stars with very different colors. One star looks blue, while the other looks orange.

1. Find the Northern Cross (Cygnus).
2. Look for the faint star at the bottom of the cross (the Swan's head). That's Albireo.

STAR STATS

LOCATION: Cygnus (SIG-nuss), the Swan

SEASON: Summer

DIFFICULTY: 2 (Medium)

SPACE FACT: A star's color is related to its temperature. The blue star of Albireo is much hotter than the orange star.

Teapot

The Teapot is another great summertime asterism. It is part of the constellation Sagittarius, the Archer. For Northern Hemisphere observers, it always appears close to the southern horizon.

1. Face south and look just above the horizon.
2. Search for a small triangle of stars sitting on top of a rectangle of stars.
3. To the left of the rectangle, a group of four stars forms the Teapot's handle. To the right, another triangle of stars makes up its spout.

STAR STATS

LOCATION: Sagittarius (saj-ih-TAIR-ee-us), the Archer

SEASON: Summer

DIFFICULTY: 2 (Medium)

SPACE FACT: The Teapot and Sagittarius are filled with star clusters and nebulae that are easy to see with binoculars and small telescopes. Just slowly pan around and you're bound to find some starry treasures.

Scorpius (the Scorpion)

SAY IT! *SCORE-pee-us*

With some imagination, the constellation Scorpius looks like a scorpion. It "crawls" across the southern sky in the summer. The scorpion's heart is the bright, orange-colored star Antares (an-TAR-eez).

1. Face south and look just above the horizon.
2. Search for the bright, orange star Antares.
3. Above or to the right of Antares, three stars form a curve. Those are the scorpion's claws.
4. From the middle claw star, trace an imaginary curving line of stars through Antares to form a hook shape. That's the scorpion's body and tail.
5. At the end of the hook, which turns upward from the horizon, two stars form the scorpion's stinger.

STAR STATS

LOCATION: Southern sky

SEASON: Summer

DIFFICULTY: 2 (Medium)

ORIGIN STORY: To ancient Greeks, Scorpius was the scorpion that killed Orion, the Hunter, with its stinger.

Pegasus (the Flying Horse)

SAY IT! *PEG-uh-sus*

You can find the constellation Pegasus, the Flying Horse, by looking for its big asterism of four stars called the Great Square.

1. Face south and look high in the sky.
2. Look for four stars, all about the same brightness, that make a large square (more than 15 degrees wide). That's the Great Square, the body of Pegasus.
3. Lines of stars stretch away from the corners of the Great Square. Those are the Flying Horse's head and legs.

STAR STATS

LOCATION: High in the southern sky

SEASON: Fall

DIFFICULTY: 2 (Medium)

SPACE FACT: Some think of the Great Square in Pegasus as a baseball diamond. There are two stars inside the square where the pitching mound might be (imagine a catcher and pitcher talking) and an umpire star behind home plate.

Andromeda Galaxy (M31)

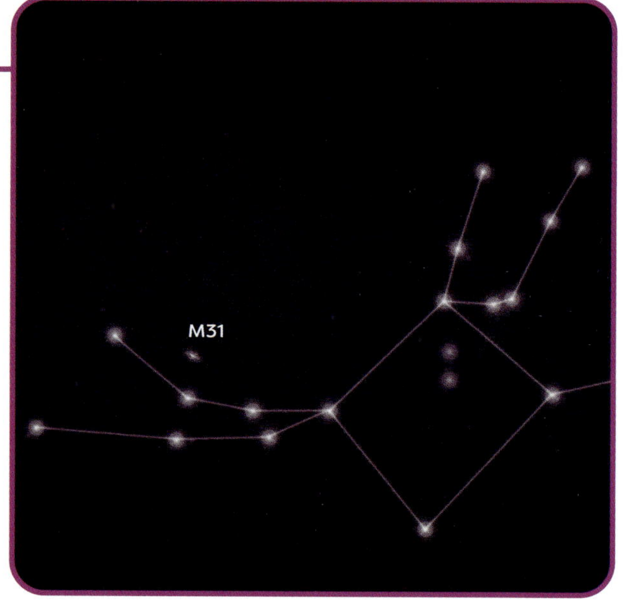

The Andromeda Galaxy is the largest galaxy close to the Milky Way. It's bright enough to see with binoculars, or even just your eyes, in a dark sky.

1. Find the Great Square in Pegasus.
2. Look for two lines of stars that make a *V* shape stretching away from one corner of the square toward the east.
3. Find the second star, away from the square, in each line.
4. Draw an imaginary line from the brighter star to the dimmer one.
5. Continue the line upward, about the same distance. The fuzzy, oval-shaped patch of light there is the Andromeda Galaxy.

STAR STATS

LOCATION: Andromeda (an-DRAH-meh-duh), the Chained Maiden

SEASON: Fall

DIFFICULTY: 3 (Hard)

SPACE FACT: The Andromeda Galaxy is slowly moving toward us. In about 5 billion years, it will collide with our galaxy!

Milky Way

This is the galaxy we live in. Because we're inside its flat disk, it looks like a faint band of clouds crossing the sky. You need a very dark sky, far from city lights, to see it.

1. On a dark summer night, find the Teapot of Sagittarius in the south.
2. Look for what appears to be steam rising out of the Teapot's spout.
3. Follow the steam high into the sky, across Cygnus, the Swan (or the Northern Cross), and down toward the northern horizon. That band of light is the Milky Way.

STAR STATS

LOCATION: Across the sky

SEASON: Visible all year, but easiest to see in the summer

DIFFICULTY: 2 (Medium)

ORIGIN STORY: The Milky Way got its name because many people thought it looked like milk spilled across the sky. Aboriginal people in Australia see an emu.

Cassiopeia (the Queen)

SAY IT! *KASS-ee-oh-PEE-ah*

Cassiopeia, the Queen, is one of the brightest and easiest-to-find constellations. Its five brightest stars form a big *W* shape in the northern sky.

1. Face north and look for the Big Dipper.
2. Use the two stars at the end of the Big Dipper's bowl to trace an imaginary line to Polaris.
3. Continue that line past Polaris about the same distance (roughly 25 degrees).
4. Look for a group of five stars forming a wide *W* (or *M*) shape. That's Cassiopeia!

STAR STATS

LOCATION: Northern sky

SEASON: Visible all year, but highest in the fall

DIFFICULTY: 1 (Easy)

ORIGIN STORY: Cassiopeia is named for a vain and boastful queen from an old Greek story. In the sky, she is sitting on her throne, which is the *W* shape of the constellation.

AROUND THE EARTH

If you are ever in the Southern Hemisphere during its summer, make sure to look for the Large Magellanic Cloud and the Small Magellanic Cloud. These are two irregular galaxies that orbit our Milky Way galaxy. They look like large and small clouds, and you can see them easily with just your eyes! They appear near each other in the southern sky and are visible all night long, depending on your latitude.

During fall in the Southern Hemisphere, a stargazer can find some well-known objects close together. First, face south and look for a group of four stars that form a small cross. That's the famous Southern Cross (the constellation Crux). To the left of the cross are two bright stars. Those are Alpha Centauri and Beta Centauri. The brighter one is Alpha Centauri, the closest star to our Sun. Alpha Centauri actually is made up of three stars that orbit each other. Also to the left of the Southern Cross, but closer to it, is a dark cloud known as the Coalsack Nebula. You can see it with just your eyes. Its dust is so thick that it blocks out the light from stars behind it.

Double Cluster

The Double Cluster is made up of two star clusters right next to each other. It is bright enough to see with your eyes in a dark sky, but it looks even better through binoculars.

1. Face north and find Cassiopeia.
2. Find the middle star of the *W* in Cassiopeia.
3. In the wider half of the *W*, look for the middle (or bottom) star in that half.
4. Draw an imaginary line through these two stars, starting from the *W*'s middle star to the other star.
5. Continue the line about 5 degrees more until you see a fuzzy patch. That's the Double Cluster.

STAR STATS

LOCATION: Perseus (PUR-see-us)

SEASON: Fall

DIFFICULTY: 2 (Medium)

SPACE FACT: Cassiopeia and the Double Cluster are high in the sky when the Big Dipper is low.

Orion (the Hunter)

SAY IT! *oh-RYE-un*

Orion, the Hunter, is one of the most famous and easiest-to-find constellations in the sky. In the winter, Orion is up all night, striding across the southern sky.

1. Face south and look for three bright stars close together in a row. That's Orion's belt.
2. Two bright stars above his belt form Orion's shoulders.
3. Two bright stars below Orion's belt form his knees (or feet).
4. If you look closely, you'll see what looks like three stars in a line hanging down from Orion's belt. That's his sword.

STAR STATS

LOCATION: Southern sky

SEASON: Winter

DIFFICULTY: 1 (Easy)

SPACE FACT: The middle "star" in Orion's sword is the Orion Nebula (M42). It is the largest star-forming region close to us. Be sure to aim your telescope at it for an amazing sight.

Betelgeuse

SAY IT! *BEE-tul-joose, BEH-tell-joose*

Betelgeuse is one of the brightest stars in the winter sky and the second-brightest star in Orion. Like some other stars, though, Betelgeuse changes brightness and can sometimes become fainter than usual. It is a super giant star—almost a thousand times bigger than the Sun! It is nearing the end of its life, and one day it will explode to produce a supernova bright enough to see from Earth.

1. In the winter, look for the three stars of Orion's belt.
2. Look to the upper left of the belt for a bright, orange star. That's Betelgeuse!

STAR STATS

LOCATION: Orion (oh-RYE-un), the Hunter

SEASON: Winter

DIFFICULTY: 1 (Easy)

ORIGIN STORY: The name Betelgeuse comes from an Arabic phrase meaning "shoulder of the giant" or, some say, "armpit of the great one"!

Rigel

SAY IT! *RYE-jel*

Rigel is the brightest star in Orion and also one of the brightest stars in the winter sky. It is a giant, blue-white star that is very hot. It gives off about twice as much heat as our Sun! Cool stars are still quite hot, and they glow like red embers. Hotter stars are white, and the hottest stars of all, like Rigel, shine blue.

1. In the winter, look for the three stars of Orion's belt.

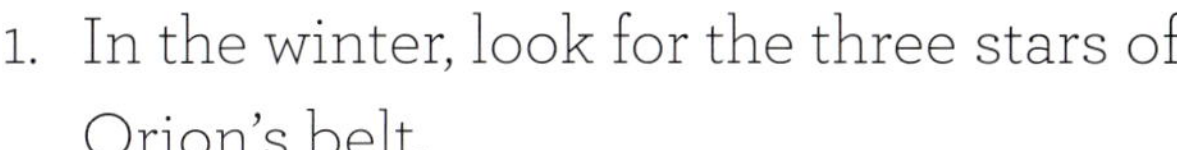

2. Look to the lower right of the belt for a bright, blue star. That's Rigel!

STAR STATS

LOCATION: Orion (oh-RYE-un), the Hunter

SEASON: Winter

DIFFICULTY: 1 (Easy)

ORIGIN STORY: The name Rigel comes from an Arabic phrase that means "the left foot of Jauzah" (the Arabic name for the constellation).

Sirius

SAY IT! *SEER-ee-us*

Sirius is the brightest star in the night sky. Sirius looks bright because it is bigger and brighter than the Sun but also because it's nearby. It is one of the closest stars to the Sun, about nine light-years away. Like all bright stars, Sirius twinkles brilliantly because of Earth's atmosphere. It's most noticeable when it is low in the sky.

1. In the winter, face south and look for Orion.
2. Draw an imaginary line through Orion's belt from right to left.
3. Keep drawing the line to the lower left of Orion until you see a very bright, blue-white star. That's Sirius!

STAR STATS

LOCATION: Canis Major (KAN-iss MAY-jor, KANE-iss MAY-jor), the Great Dog

SEASON: Winter

DIFFICULTY: 1 (Easy)

SPACE FACT: Sirius is also known as the Dog Star because it's the brightest star in Canis Major, the Great Dog.

Canis Major (the Great Dog)

SAY IT! *KAN-iss MAY-jor, KANE-iss MAY-jor*

Canis Major is a constellation near Orion. It is also known as the Great Dog. It is one of Orion's two hunting dogs that follow that constellation through the sky. The other is Canis Minor, the Small Dog.

1. Face south and find Sirius, the brightest star in the night sky.
2. Sirius is the Dog's chest. Look for a long line of stars behind Sirius (away from Orion) that forms the Dog's body and tail. Two stars below that line form the Dog's legs.

STAR STATS

LOCATION: Southern sky

SEASON: Winter

DIFFICULTY: 2 (Medium)

ORIGIN STORY: Canis Major is Orion's largest hunting dog. It chases the constellation Lepus, the Hare, through the sky every winter night.

Hyades

SAY IT! *HIGH-ah-deez*

The Hyades is a large star cluster. It is also one of the closest star clusters to us. All the stars in the Hyades were born around the same time. Because it's big and spread out, it's a good cluster to explore with binoculars or a small telescope.

1. In the winter, face south and find Orion.
2. Look to the right of Orion for a very bright, orange star. That's Aldebaran (all-DEB-er-on), the brightest star in the constellation Taurus, the Bull.
3. Look just below (or to the right of) Aldebaran for a *V*-shaped group of fainter stars. That group is the Hyades.

STAR STATS

LOCATION: Taurus (TOR-us), the Bull

SEASON: Winter

DIFFICULTY: 2 (Medium)

SPACE FACT: The Hyades forms the face of the constellation Taurus. Aldebaran is the Bull's gleaming eye.

Pleiades (the Seven Sisters, M45)

SAY IT! *PLEE-ah-deez*

The Pleiades are a bright cluster of stars. They are often called the Seven Sisters. Even though you can see only six stars with just your eyes, you can see many more with binoculars or a telescope.

1. In the winter, face south and look for Orion.
2. Draw an imaginary line through Orion's belt from left to right, and keep drawing the line all the way through the Hyades until you reach a small group of bright, blue-white stars. It looks almost like a mini-dipper. You've found the Pleiades!

STAR STATS

LOCATION: Taurus (TOR-us), the Bull

SEASON: Winter

DIFFICULTY: 1 (Easy)

SPACE FACT: These stars are only about 100 million years old. They formed much more recently than everything in our Solar System, which is about 5 billion years old. The Pleiades are about 400 light-years away.

Crab Nebula (M1)

The Crab Nebula is a cloud of gas blasted out by a huge star when it exploded as a supernova. When you look through binoculars or a small telescope, it looks like a fuzzy star.

1. Find Aldebaran and the *V* shape of the Hyades.
2. Draw an imaginary line from the bottom of the *V* through Aldebaran.
3. Keep going until you reach a medium-bright star.
4. Aim your telescope about 1 degree north of that star and look for a fuzzy object. That's the Crab Nebula.

STAR STATS

LOCATION: Taurus (TOR-us), the Bull

SEASON: Winter

DIFFICULTY: 3 (Hard)

SPACE FACT: In the year 1054, stargazers around the world saw the supernova that created the Crab Nebula. It was so bright, people could see it in the daytime!

HOW TO VIEW AN ECLIPSE

Lunar and solar eclipses are amazing sights! A lunar eclipse happens when the Moon passes into Earth's shadow, making it darken or turn red. All you need to watch a lunar eclipse is your eyes.

A solar eclipse happens when the Moon covers up some or all of the Sun from our view. But even when part of the Sun is covered during an eclipse, it is too bright to look at directly—unless you have a safe solar filter to block out most of the sunlight. You can wear special eclipse glasses with filters in them.

You can also make what is called a pinhole projector with just two pieces of paper or cardboard. Poke a small hole in one piece with a pin or a tack. With your back to the Sun, hold that piece up and let sunlight shine onto the other piece. You'll see a picture of the Sun on it!

Gemini (the Twins)

SAY IT! *JEM-in-eye*

Gemini, the Twins, is a constellation with two bright stars next to each other, named Castor (KASS-tur) and Pollux (PAH-lux). Other stars in the constellation form what looks like two stick figures standing next to each other. Castor and Pollux are their heads.

1. Find Rigel and Betelgeuse in the constellation Orion.
2. Draw an imaginary line from Rigel to Betelgeuse.
3. Continue drawing that line up past Betelgeuse, about one-and-a-half times the distance between Rigel and Betelgeuse.
4. You should see two bright stars side by side. Those are Castor and Pollux, Gemini's two brightest stars.

STAR STATS

LOCATION: Southern sky

SEASON: Winter

DIFFICULTY: 2 (Medium)

SPACE FACT: Castor is actually a group of six stars. You can easily see two of Castor's stars with a small telescope.

Craters on Earth's Moon

When you look at the Moon, the large, dark areas are "seas" of frozen lava called maria (MAR-ee-ah). Craters look like round holes punched into the surface. They form when space rocks hit the Moon. Big craters have long, bright lines streaking away from them called rays. These lines are material blasted out when the crater formed.

1. Check websites, apps, computer programs, or astronomy magazines to find out when the Moon will be up. (Or just go outside and look for it!)
2. Aim your telescope at the Moon. (Warning: it might be bright.)
3. Search for circles or round shapes on the Moon. Those are craters.

STAR STATS

LOCATION: Ecliptic

DIFFICULTY: 1 (Easy)

SPACE FACT: During the month, the Moon changes shape, or goes through "phases." When the Moon is crescent shaped or not yet full, craters along its lit edge can look especially dramatic through a telescope.

Mercury

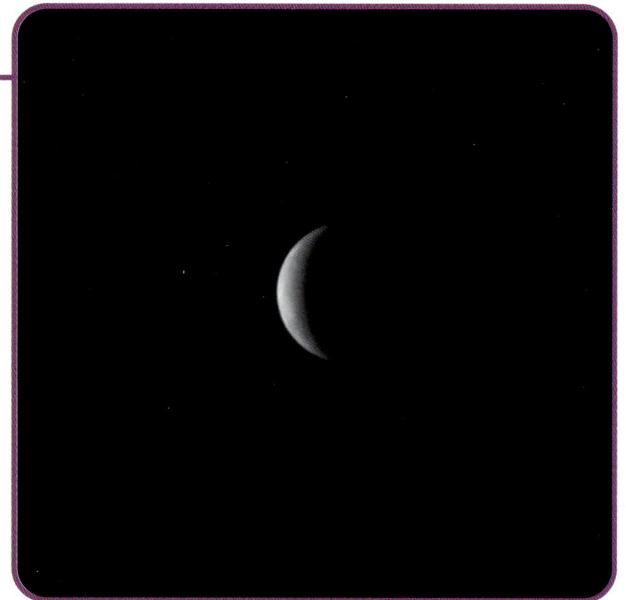

SAY IT! *MER-cure-ee*

Mercury is the smallest planet and the closest to the Sun. In fact, Mercury is often too close to the Sun to see. When it's far enough away, you have just a short time to spot it after sunset or before sunrise.

1. Check astronomy magazines, websites, apps, or computer programs to find out where and when to see Mercury.
2. If it's up in the evening, face west after sunset and search for what looks like a faint star. If it's up in the morning, face east before sunrise and look for it there.
3. If you aim a telescope at it, Mercury will look like a small white object that's bigger than a star.

STAR STATS

LOCATION: Ecliptic

DIFFICULTY: 2 (Medium)

SPACE FACT: Mercury has phases, like the Moon! You can see it changing shape between crescent, gibbous, and full with a big-enough telescope.

Venus

SAY IT! *VEE-nus*

Venus is the second planet from the Sun. It's bigger, brighter, and often farther from the Sun than Mercury is, making it easier to find. Its phases are easier to see than Mercury's, too. Sometimes, Venus is brighter than every star in the night sky.

1. Check astronomy magazines, websites, apps, or computer programs to find out when to see Venus.
2. If it's up in the evening, search for what looks like a bright star in the west after sunset. If it's up in the morning, look east before sunrise.
3. Through a telescope, Venus will look like a small white circle or crescent.

STAR STATS

LOCATION: Ecliptic

DIFFICULTY: 1 (Easy)

SPACE FACT: Some call Venus the "morning star" or "evening star" because it shines before sunrise or after sunset.

Mars

SAY IT! *MARZ*

Mars is one of the smallest planets in our Solar System, but it is also one of the closest to Earth. Like Earth, Mars has white ice caps at its poles. With a good telescope, you might be able to see them. Also keep a lookout for dark features on the planet's surface.

1. Check astronomy magazines, websites, apps, or computer programs to find out when and where to see Mars in the sky.
2. Face south and look for a reddish or orangish "star" that doesn't twinkle.
3. Aim your telescope at that "star." If your telescope reveals a small, orangish, circular disk, you've found Mars!

STAR STATS

LOCATION: Ecliptic

DIFFICULTY: 2 (Medium)

ORIGIN STORY: Mars is named after the Roman god of war.

Jupiter

SAY IT! *JOO-pih-tur*

Jupiter is the largest planet in our Solar System and one of the most interesting planets to look at through a telescope. With a good telescope and a clear, dark sky, you can see brown bands of clouds crossing the planet. With a big-enough telescope, you might even make out the planet's monster storm, the Great Red Spot.

1. Check astronomy magazines, websites, apps, or computer programs to find out where and when to see Jupiter in the sky.
2. Face south and look for a bright, yellowish-white "star" that doesn't twinkle.
3. Aim your telescope at that "star." If your telescope shows you a yellowish-white circular object with brown stripes, you've found Jupiter!

STAR STATS

LOCATION: Ecliptic

DIFFICULTY: 1 (Easy)

SPACE FACT: By studying pictures of Jupiter taken over many years, astronomers have discovered that Jupiter's Great Red Spot is shrinking!

Galilean Moons

SAY IT! *GAL-ih-LAY-un*

The Galilean moons are the four largest and brightest moons of Jupiter: Io, Europa, Ganymede, and Callisto. Italian astronomer Galileo Galilei discovered them in 1610. He was one of the first people to ever look at the night sky with a telescope. When he discovered these moons, it showed that some things in the heavens did not orbit Earth, which shocked many people.

1. Find Jupiter and aim your telescope at it.
2. Look for what appear to be stars next to Jupiter. Those "stars" are the Galilean moons! (Since they move around depending on the time of year, you'll probably see them in a different order than in the photo above.)

STAR STATS

LOCATION: Ecliptic, next to Jupiter

DIFFICULTY: 2 (Medium)

SPACE FACT: You can't always spot all four moons at once. Sometimes they hide in front of or behind Jupiter. Try viewing them several nights in a row and sketching how their positions change, just like Galileo did.

Saturn and Its Rings

SAY IT! *SAT-urn*

Saturn is one of four giant planets in our Solar System with rings, but its rings are the biggest and brightest. Saturn's rings are actually made of bits of rock and ice. Gaps appear between some rings. You can see the largest gap with a good telescope.

1. Check astronomy magazines, websites, apps, or computer programs to find out where and when to see Saturn in the sky.
2. Face south and look for a bright, yellowish or orangish "star" that doesn't twinkle.
3. Aim your telescope at that "star." When you see a circular object that has two lobes sticking out of it, that's Saturn!

STAR STATS

LOCATION: Ecliptic

DIFFICULTY: 1 (Easy)

SPACE FACT: When Galileo first looked at Saturn through his telescope in 1610, he didn't know what the rings were. He called them "ears."

Uranus

SAY IT! *YER-ih-nus*

Uranus is one of the largest planets in our Solar System. But because it is so far away, it looks like a very dim star. You will probably need binoculars or a telescope to spot it, and you will need to know exactly where to look.

1. Check astronomy magazines, websites, apps, or computer programs to find out where and when to see Uranus in the sky.
2. Face south and aim your telescope where Uranus should be.
3. If you see a small, pale green, circular object through your telescope, you've found Uranus!

STAR STATS

LOCATION: Ecliptic

DIFFICULTY: 3 (Hard)

ORIGIN STORY: After he discovered Uranus in 1781, astronomer William Herschel wanted to name it *Georgium Sidus* ("George's star" in Latin) after the king of England. Instead, Uranus is named after the Greek god of the sky.

Neptune

SAY IT! *NEP-toon*

Of the eight planets in the Solar System, Neptune is the farthest from the Sun (and from Earth). Neptune is also the smallest of the giant planets. So it is too faint to see with just your eyes. You will need binoculars or a telescope to spot Neptune, and you will need to know exactly where to find it. If you do, you might see its biggest moon, Triton, nearby.

1. Check astronomy magazines, websites, apps, or computer programs to find out where and when to see Neptune in the sky.
2. Face south and aim your telescope where Neptune should be.
3. If you see a small, blue, circular object through your telescope, you've found Neptune!

STAR STATS

LOCATION: Ecliptic

DIFFICULTY: 3 (Hard)

ORIGIN STORY: Blue-colored Neptune is named after the Roman god of the sea.

MORE TO DISCOVER

RECOMMENDED WEBSITES, APPS, MAGAZINES, AND BOOKS

STELLARIUM (STELLARIUM.ORG)
This free program (and app) will show you what the sky looks like on any date, at any time, anywhere in the world. Another popular program is Starry Night.

SKYVIEW LITE
This free app is one of many that show you what's in the sky in whatever direction you aim a phone or tablet. Similar apps include Star Walk, SkySafari, Star Chart, and Night Sky.

HEAVENS-ABOVE (HEAVENS-ABOVE.COM)
The website and app will tell you when you can see the International Space Station or other satellites pass overhead. Enter your location and get a list of satellites you can see tonight.

THE SKY LIVE (THESKYLIVE.COM)
This website is a good place to find out what planets, comets, asteroids, and other objects are in your sky tonight.

THE AMERICAN METEOR SOCIETY (AMSMETEORS.ORG)
This group's website lists meteor showers and when they are visible during the year, along with other information about shooting stars.

NIGHT SKY NETWORK (NIGHTSKY.JPL.NASA.GOV)
This NASA website can help you find astronomy clubs and events in your area. The Astronomical League is another group for astronomy clubs.

ASTRONOMY **MAGAZINE (ASTRONOMY.COM)**

This magazine and its website share equipment reviews, sky maps highlighting interesting things to look at, and articles about astronomy. Another popular magazine (and website) is *Sky & Telescope* (SkyAndTelescope.org).

THE STARS **BY H. A. REY**

In this book, learn even more about stars and constellations, find star charts for every season, and discover how and why things move in the sky.

GLOSSARY

ASTERISM: (ASS-ter-is-um) A group of stars that forms a shape or pattern but is not a constellation

ASTEROID: A rocky object in our Solar System that's smaller than a planet and orbits the Sun

ATMOSPHERE: The layers of gas surrounding a planet or moon

COMET: An object made of ice and rock that sheds gas and dust, producing a tail, when it's heated by the Sun

CONSTELLATION: A region of the sky with a group of stars that often seems to form a shape or pattern

DEGREE: A unit of measurement across the sky; there are 360 degrees in a circle

ECLIPTIC: (ee-KLIP-tick) The path through the sky that the Sun, Moon, and planets travel along during the year

FOCUS: To turn something from blurry to clear

GALAXY: A collection of stars, dust, and gas, all held together by gravity

GAS: A collection of atoms that isn't dense enough to form a liquid or solid

GRAVITY: An invisible force that pulls things together

HORIZON: A place in the distance where the sky and ground appear to meet

LIGHT-YEAR: The distance that light travels in one year (about 5.9 trillion miles or 9.5 trillion kilometers)

MAGNIFICATION: The process of making something look bigger, or the number of times bigger something looks through this process (a magnification of 10 means the object looks 10 times bigger than usual)

MAGNITUDE: The brightness of an object in the sky, described as a number; the brightest objects have low numbers, and the dimmest objects have high numbers

METEOR: A streak of light created in the sky when a small space rock enters Earth's atmosphere and burns up; also called a shooting star

METEOR SHOWER: An event when a lot of meteors appear on the same night; several meteor showers happen every year

MOON: A natural object that orbits a planet or asteroid

NEBULA: (NEB-yoo-lah) A large cloud of gas and dust in space

NORTHERN LIGHTS: A colorful glow in the sky created when particles from the Sun collide with Earth's atmosphere; also called aurorae

PLANET: A large, round body in space that orbits the Sun or another star

PLANISPHERE: (PLAN-iss-fear) A map of the night sky that can be turned like a dial to show what stars and constellations are in the sky on a given day or at a given time

SATELLITE: An object that orbits another object, such as those that orbit Earth, like spacecraft and the Moon

STAR: A huge ball of glowing gas, held together by gravity

STAR CLUSTER: A group of stars that all formed together around the same time and are held together by gravity

SUN: The star at the center of our Solar System

SUPERNOVA: The explosion of a massive star, which makes the star look much brighter in the sky from Earth for a short time

UNIVERSE: All of time and space and everything that has ever existed in it

INDEX

T

U

V

W

Z

ABOUT THE AUTHOR

Vanessa Thomas is a writer who loves astronomy. She grew up in Michigan and fell in love with the stars on camping trips with her family. She studied astronomy and science writing at the Massachusetts Institute of Technology.

During her career, Vanessa has worked as a science writer for the Hubble Space Telescope at NASA, and has written articles for science websites and magazines, including *Astronomy* and *Sky & Telescope*.

Today she is the public information officer for the National Optical-Infrared Astronomy Research Laboratory (NOIRLab), where she writes about the discoveries made by large telescopes in Arizona, Hawaii, and Chile.

Vanessa is an amateur astronomer, visiting dark sites to explore the sky with her telescopes and binoculars. She enjoys sharing views through her telescope with others. She loves traveling the world to witness total solar eclipses, and has seen five so far (in five different countries).